Least to Most Loved

Jacqueline Navarrete

BookLeaf Publishing
India | USA | UK

Presentation by *BookLeaf Publishing*

Web: www.bookleafpub.com

E-mail: info@bookleafpub.com

ISBN: 978-93-5744-995-3

First edition 2022

DEDICATION

To everyone who has helped get me to where I am now. I love you!

Special Mentions to:

MVSharpe

Kay Ford

Lisa Guzman Navarrete

Jeana Schweikhard

Jacqueline Navarrete

Jackie Navarrete

ACKNOWLEDGEMENT

I acknowledge myself because I do not get acknowledged enough.

:)

PREFACE

Dear Me,

Just know that this project symbolizes who you
are.
You will one day be brave to publish those
forbidden and deleted poems.
I love you!

Dear Me

What you will see in life will look like a black
hole,
will feel like a lonely winter night,
will smell like vinegar,
will sound like the pin that drops in an empty
room.
Unwanted. Loud.
Inconvenient.

This will be your beginning.

You will be a burden to yourself and others.

As you become flesh in the world, know that
each day you will fight that same flesh to leave
this world.

However, you will decide which path you take.

Don't worry after a few missteps, you will take
the right one.

Sadness

Sadness consumes me in a wind of doubt.

She hides behind a mask caked with lies.

She comforts me when the mask fades.

She never fails to remind me to put the mask on.

She is shy.

Don't let them see me.
They won't understand.
They will tear me apart.
Put the mask back on.

Oh, Sadness.

She has been with me longer than anyone in my life.

Hope

Isn't it funny how life works.
In the void of darkness, where all seems lost,
It takes a drop of light to illuminate a whole lost
world.

The 'A' Word

A word so vague as if to make sure it is so faint
that it looses the pain it brings with it.

A word so destructive, it can break even the
strongest wills.

A word so permanent it lingers everywhere:
mind, body, heart, and soul.

A word so embarrassing it assures it stays
hidden.

A word so many are afraid of.

A word many see.

A word that sting.

A word that too often draws blood.

A word that too often takes lives.

It's time to end it's power.

It's time to make that power ours.

It's time to yell A-B-U-S-E

With our heads held high and body healing.

Stone Cold

Your tears,
so dark that they touched my pink, fresh,
youthful, carefree heart and turned it stone cold.

Why would you do that?

I don't think I asked for much, dad.

People Pleasing

I can feel it even now.
The anticipation of overflowing happiness.
The preparation.
The delivery.

Everything perfect.

But it always seems to catch me off guard.

The rejection.

The indifference which sinks my heart to the pit
of my stomach, and yet as if not wanting to fall
alone, my heart reaches up and attempts to pull a
tear with it.

But with one deep breath, which stabs my heart,
and a half smile that finishes the job,
I forget the anticipation, the preparation, and the
delivery.

I keep it moving with a heart that will take time
to repair
with a heart who will always be ready for the
anticipation, the preparation, and the delivery,

with a heart who will always forget to factor in
the anticipation.

Shift 1

Sadness hid, and passion erupted.

Dreams.

Passion erupts in me like a volcano.
It is the fuel that gets me out of bed.
It is what keeps me alive.
It is where I found purpose.

It awakened in me something dormant.

Suddenly, I became the princess and the fairytale
was about me reaching my destination. No step
too big. No challenge too great.

Each step developed within it a story meant only
for those who dreamed with their eyes open.

The Cycle

Who was I to break the cycle?

No-one had ever beaten the cycle.

Yet, Who am I not to.

Fifth Period

Okaaaaaay, fiiiiifth periiiiiiod

It was the only way to get their attention.

Absolutely nowhere in my education or training had they prepared me for fifth period. 32 of them. 22 of them boys. After lunch.

And me, a first year teacher.

This is the year it felt like I would almost run out of love, and just just justtt when I was showing 'E' fifth period would come in and refill my heart.

Hall Walker

Hall walker
Hall walker
Where do you go?

Hall walker
Hall walker
What do you see?

Hall walker
Hall walker
How do you feel?

Hall walker
Hall walker
Let me hold you, dear.

Hall walker
Hall walker
We are in this for you!

Hall walker
Hall walker
Can you see what we see?

Hall walker

Hall walker
Untapped potential.

Hall walker
Hall walker
You have it in you.

Hall walker
Hall walker
Come rest.

Hall walker
Hall walker
We know you want to try your best.

Hall walker
Hall walker
Let me join you for one step, and all the rest.

Shift 2

Sadness Hid, Passion Erupted, and I Rooted and Bloomed.

Nourishment

I often remember the Jews newly freed from
concentration camps.
A ghost of a man, and a faint image of a body.

They must have been eager to be free.

But although liberated, many died shortly after.

The soldiers killed them.

Not purposefully, but out of love.

When they saw these men worked to nothing
more than a thin layer of skin and bones, they
began to feed them their rations.

But a body unaccustomed to an overflowing of
food goes into shock, and shock led to death.

The soldiers had to, against their will, take away
the food- which might as well be the
equivalence of happiness for those Jews.

I think of this story because of the parallel I see
in my own life.

A desperation to reach something so precious.
A desperation to reach something so common.

In my desperation, I was able to rejoice in the
overflow.

I came to the kingdom of God starved of love.
I found Him and it was an endless buffet of love,
mercy, patience, and kindness.
It was a well which contained the sweetest
water; water that came inside and made way for
the nourishment of love.
Never ending water that opened up each crease
and made a way for love to sneak in.

The more I took in, the more I began to truly
live.

Hide and Seek

Like a game of hide and seek
You came to find me

Hidden in plain sight, I hid

Not knowing who you were leaving behind.

Such childish games.

I did not want to hide.
But I was not worthy of being found.

You could imagine my surprise when you found
my heart,
lifted my head,
put a crown on it, and
carried me to safety.

Tool

Even though you think you know, you could not
even begin to know especially not understand

Reminder

Stop making/controlling the plan,
let God lead you,
stay planted and grow.

My purpose is to be used, so I have to allow it

Utilize us for a better work, God

A mother holds her child closer to her heart than
herself.
We know by history that using our voice is not
always the best way to have a good outcome. We
see how change ends up happening with one
voice and one face, but that voice is often built
of other people's voices heard too loudly or too
soon.

Why a mother would ask her son to use his
voice is intriguing to me because she
understands that even though she might be

setting her child up to face persecution, she is
ultimately setting her son up to do what really
matters in this world: impacting.

God is asking us to CRY OUT to those who
don't know Him yet.
He is asking us to CRY OUT for those who have
gone astray.
He is asking us to CRY OUT for those who are
to weak to cry out for themselves. He is asking
us to CRY OUT for those who are worn from
crying out themselves. He is asking us to CRY
OUT for those who can't or haven't found their
own CRY!

Although we might face danger when we CRY
OUT,
I can't stand to think of what my life would be if
someone did not CRY OUT for me-How the
Good News would have reached me.

And now, I have a chance to be that vessel, those
vocal cords, those triumphantly loud prayers,
and those victorious quiet and intimate prayers.

It is only with VOICE that we can change; it is
only with VOICE that we can disciple.

What makes voice the most astonishing is that
Voice IS NOT always audible but it is always
audible.

Foundation

Wisdom is necessary.
Understanding must be established.
Knowledge must be present.
To build anything.

Wisdom

I have always said I have a faulty foundation
because of my parents and my overall
upbringing,
but that is not valid anymore.

Knowing that, I take that burden and put it in
God's hands.

Everyday he is equipping me with knowledge
and knowledge has to be understood and applied
to make me rich in wisdom,
when I fully obey and allow more of him and
less of me, then I and others will begin to see my
fortress, my palace, my place of devotion to the
Lord all sitting on God's strong and mighty
foundation. Amen!

Control It

Your Self control affects who you are.

Warning

Self control is so hard to do
We have to have control to go against our flesh
We have to have control to not back lash at
people
Not over eat
To eat the right things
To read our word instead
To pray instead of worry
To walk in faith

But those of us who lack self control will have
gaps of faith and gaps of the flesh

Self control is necessary

Nothing will remain in you, if you do not have
it.

Rely on Him.

Pain

Being tamed by the Word of God will spare you.

This was written as a warning.

The tools used on the animals are tools used when they are wild and uncontrollable.

A rod on the fools back symbolizes much more than just a rod.

I cannot remember the last time someone hit me with a rod. But because I know that the Word Must be applicable to me, I know that the rod on the fools back symbolizes pain.

And that pain can be lost opportunities, failed businesses, even goals that are not achieved, loss of someone dear to us, or just anything that causes us pain.

Therefore, if we do not conform to God's Word as believers, then we are allowing and inviting pain into our lives.

Emotional pain, spiritual pain, physical pain, mental pain, and all because we want to live in our own will.

I have to make sure that I am not running around like a wild animal, I have to make sure that my actions are being sharpened and molded through and by God's word.

It's funny how you can memorize the verse but not live it.

In the spiritual we see the whole picture.

Stay Put.

Stay in your place and let God be your base.

Warning

A bird that leaves his nest is in danger.
A bird that leaves its nest to quickly is pretty much dead, because they don't have the adaptations needed or the skills needed to survive in the world.
A bird that leaves his nest could be looking for food or just enjoying the day, and at the time it sounds like a good idea, but the danger is still there.

So our placement, can be anywhere.

Our place could be our home; our place could be our car; our place could be our workplace, but our place is not on earth.

Our rightful place is not on earth.

Our rightful place is at God's feet.

Because our rightful place is being God-fearing, when we leave God's feet no matter the situation, we are setting ourselves up for danger to attack us.

And as we know danger could be anything from humans to supernatural warfare attacks on our spirit.

We should not think of our place as somewhere on earth, we should think about our place in terms of where our heart is.

Because God is not asking us to stay put forever in one place, he is asking that we take the place that we hold him in our heart everywhere.

Stay put.

Don't leave his side.

Carry him always. He wants to be with you!

The Ultimate
Prayer.

Dear God,

Save me from myself.
I rest it all in you.
Thank you for loving me today and always.

Amen

Sadness Part 2

Hello old friend.
Can you see my mask is no more.

Sadness,
Can you see I found me?

Sadness,
Will you depart from me?

Sadness,
It's been too long.

Sadness,
You are too dark, and I have found my light.